The Royal Mile

Text by Tom Bruce-Gardyne

Photographs by Colin Baxter

Colin Baxter Photography Ltd, Grantown-on-Spey, Scotland

The Royal Mile

Edinburgh Castle
sits atop the Castle Rock, an ancient volcano. There is evidence of occupation on this site dating back some 3000 years. Home of Scotland's kings and queens in medieval times, today the Castle houses Scotland's Crown Jewels and the Stone of Destiny. St Margaret's Chapel, built in the 12th century, is the oldest building in the Castle.

Cannonball House
Believed to have been built by a furrier called Mure in 1630, it got its name from a cannonball lodged in the west gable of the house. According to legend, the ball was fired from a cannon on the Half Moon Battery in 1745, when the Castle held out for George II against Bonnie Prince Charlie.

Riddle's Court dates back to 1587 and was named after George Riddell, wright and burgess of the city. Later the City Treasurer, Bailie John McMorran, lived here until shot dead in 1595 by boys at the High School [now the Scotch Whisky Heritage Centre] in a dispute over school holidays.

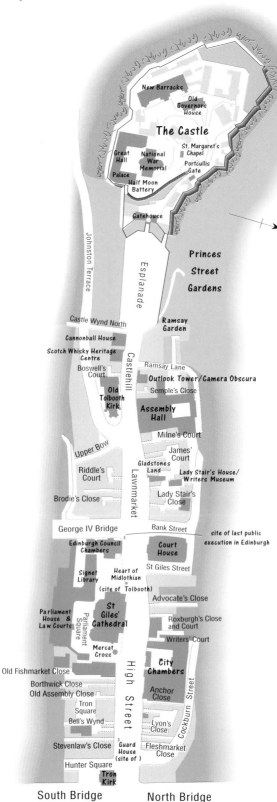

The Camera Obscura
opened to the public in 1853 and uses a periscope to project a bird's-eye view of the city onto a wide dish. Some early viewers were apparently so startled that they fainted.

James' Court,
built on the site of an earlier close, by the developer, James Brownhill, in 1725. It was home to the famous Scottish philosopher, David Hume, and later to Sir Patrick Geddes, the 19th century 'father of town planning'.

City Chambers
Designed by John Adam in 1753 as a Royal Exchange, a place for merchants, lawyers and others to do business, it had become the Town Council by 1811. At 12 storeys high it is one of the tallest buildings remaining in the Old Town.

South Bridge

North Bridge

High Street

Niddry Street

Carrubber's Close

Old St Paul's Church

North Gray's Close

Blackfriar's Street

Bailie Fyfe's Close

Paisley Close

Chalmers' Close

South Gray's Close

John Knox House

Museum of Childhood

Trunk's Close

Moubray House

Netherbow Arts Centre

Tweeddale Court

World's End Close

Netherbow Port (site of)

Jeffrey Street

St.Mary's Street

Cranston St.

Gullan's Close

(Mid Common Close/ site of Morocco Land)

Chessels Court

New Street

Old Playhouse Close

Canongate

St.John's Street

Moray House

Bible Land/ Shoemaker's Land

→ N

Old Tolbooth Wynd

Museum of Edinburgh

Canongate Tolbooth/ The People's Story

Bakehouse Close

Canongate Kirk and Kirkyard

Acheson House

Dunbar's Close Garden

Panmure Close

Scottish Poetry Library

Lochend Close

Bull's Close

Canongate

Reid's Court

Jenny Ha's

Brown's Close (site of Golfer's Land)

Reid's Close

Whitefoord House

Queensberry House

White Horse Close

White Horse Inn

The Scottish Parliament

Horse Wynd

Abbey Strand

Abbeyhill Crescent

The Queen's Gallery

Palace Gates

Palace of Holyroodhouse

Holyrood Abbey

yards 275 — 250 metres

220 — 200

165 — 150

110 — 100

55 — 50

0 — 0

Moubray House
is said to be one of the oldest houses in the city, with origins dating back to around 1450. The writer Daniel Defoe, lived here in the early 18th century and was apparently pelted with stones and rubbish when he looked out of the window for being a suspected English spy.

Old Playhouse Close
This was the site of Edinburgh's first theatre, built in 1746, and connected to the Royal Mile by an old 16th-century close. It was later home to the writer Tobias Smollett.

Moray House
was built in about 1625 by the Dowager Countess of Home, and named after her daughter, the Countess of Moray. In the gardens, the final signatures to the Treaty of Union were added in 1707.

The Scottish Parliament
Construction of the new Scottish Parliament building began in 1999, on a site opposite the Palace of Holyroodhouse. The building was designed by Spanish architect Enric Miralles. The complex includes a debating chamber, committee rooms, offices for MSPs and facilities for visitors.

The Palace of Holyroodhouse,
the official residence in Scotland of the British monarch, was begun in 1501 by James IV, who moved the royal court from the Castle to the Palace. It was extended by James V around 1530, and largely rebuilt after a fire in 1650.

White Horse Close
This was the original stables of Holyroodhouse and the Close was named after Mary Queen of Scots' white palfrey. It later became a Jacobite HQ during the '45 rebellion, and then a famous Inn and terminus of stage-coaches to London – a journey of eight days in 1754.

Holyrood Abbey
was founded by David I in 1128 and completed in 1141. The present ruins of a much larger building date from the late 12th and early 13th centuries. In the 17th century the nave was the Chapel Royal of the Order of the Knights of the Thistle, founded by James VII in 1687. Much of the building collapsed in 1768.

The Royal Mile

'Stately Edinburgh, thronged on crags,' declared William Wordsworth as he gazed upon the city's famously dramatic outline. One can imagine the eyes of the great poet sweeping down from the surrounding hills, following the outline of the rooftops, chimney-pots and steeples before settling on the Castle itself. Some 150 years after his death, it is still impossible not to be drawn to the towering

clifftop fortress at the heart of Edinburgh. It continues to dominate the skyline from all sides, especially when silhouetted against the evening sky, or floodlit at night.

To climb up to the Castle's battlements and peer down gives a wonderful perspective on the city, and also helps demonstrate how Edinburgh has been fashioned by nature from the very start. For most of its history, this was a cramped hilltop town, with a sheer drop to the west and steep valleys on either side. Given such constraints, the only option as the city began to expand was to build eastwards from the Castle, site of the earliest settlement, along the narrow ridge that sloped down to the sea and the twelfth-century Abbey of Holyrood. At the same time, from the opposite direction, buildings began to climb up the hill from Holyrood. When the two met, in the sixteenth century, to complete a single street 1984 yards long, the Royal Mile was born.

Standing in front of the Castle today it is hard to believe this was once the scene of violent volcanic activity, especially if one is being whipped raw by the east wind, which is often the way. Around 340 million years ago, however, white-hot lava oozed up from deep beneath one's feet to form a giant cone, taller and much wider than

The Palace of Holyroodhouse (above), The Castle & Royal Mile from the air (right)

the present hill. Then came the ice age with its glaciers moving west to east, pummelling into the soft layers of outer rock to expose the by-now extinct volcano's inner core. This is the fist of black basalt rock that the Castle sits on. As the glaciers ploughed on they left thousands of tons of sediment in their wake, forming a perfect example of what geologists call a 'crag and tail'.

In Edinburgh the tail trails eastwards from the Castle rock for an old Scottish mile, 100 yards (92 metres) longer than an imperial mile, until it reaches the flat.

Writers throughout the ages have likened the city's most famous street to an animal – a huge lizard, a turtle, a flat fish, even a rhinoceros – and it is not hard to see why. The Royal Mile, with its hundreds of narrow side streets, or closes, jutting out like ribs on either side, forms an obvious backbone. Before the late eighteenth century, when Edinburgh burst its Old Town banks to create the Georgian New Town, almost all life in the city revolved around this single street. Today it is hard to walk down it without feeling the deep imprint of history. Who knows? – perhaps some future ice age will remove all trace of Edinburgh, and when the glaciers retreat the city's old spine will be revealed, embedded in the rock like a fossil.

The Castle, Esplanade & Castlehill

There is evidence from recent excavations to show that the site where the Castle now stands was occupied some 3000 years ago, with traces of forts from the Iron and the Dark Ages. The Castle itself first appears in written records in the eleventh century, when it was the home of kings, from Malcolm III and his queen, Margaret, in whose memory the oldest building in the Castle, St Margaret's Chapel, was built in the twelfth century. Today there are buildings old and new within the Castle walls, including the Great Hall, used on ceremonial

occasions, the Palace which houses the Crown Room, where the Honours of Scotland (Scottish crown jewels) are displayed, as well as a more modern restaurant and shops.

Given its position 440 ft (134 m) above sea-level, and the thickness of its walls, the occupants of the Castle must have felt secure, if not complacent, against the threat of attack. Yet ever since the English first took the Castle in 1174 and held it for 12 years, it seldom enjoyed a moment's peace. It was again captured by King Edward I in 1296 and held until the Earl of Moray somehow scaled the north face and drove the English out in 1314. As a result, King Robert the Bruce, whose crown is on display in the Castle beside the Stone of Destiny, was reinstated. To provide better protection, two siege guns were hauled up here in 1457, including the massive Mons Meg which could blast a 500 lb (227 kg) ball of granite up to 2 miles (3 km). In the sixteenth century the half-moon battery was added, but neither cannons nor ramparts were enough to keep out Cromwell's New Model Army in 1650, or the Protestant army of William of Orange in 1689.

The Castle esplanade, the nineteenth-century parade ground, forms the stage for the annual Military Tattoo, a highlight of the Edinburgh Festival. On the northeast corner is Ramsay Garden, a large block of flats that bulges

outwards, almost spilling over the precipice. It was built in 1893 by the renowned conservationist and town-planner Patrick Geddes, who did more than anyone to rescue the Royal Mile from its centuries of neglect. Behind Ramsay Garden, on Castlehill, stands a curious tower that looks like a lighthouse. If you look closely you can just discern a small pipe protruding from the white, domed roof. This is the Outlook Tower and the pipe is in fact a periscope, which gives a wonderful bird's eye view of the city projected through a series of lenses and mirrors onto a large white dish. When Maria Theresa Short opened her Camera Obscura to the public in

1853, it was too much for some; with the invention of moving pictures a long way off, the idea of people, carriages and clouds moving across a screen caused one or two to faint.

Opposite stands the old Castlehill School, now the Scotch Whisky Heritage Centre, where you can sit in a plastic barrel and be taken on a 'virtual tour' through 300 years of whisky-making history. It also acts as an embassy to the industry's far-flung distilleries. Next door is Boswell's Court, named after the uncle of James Boswell, who is believed to have stayed here with Dr Samuel Johnson in 1773 before the two set off on their great tour

The Outlook Tower & Old Tolbooth Kirk dominate the view towards Arthur's Seat

of the Hebrides. In its time it has housed the Edinburgh Hellfire Club, been a committee room for the Church of Scotland and is now the Witchery Restaurant.

A little further on stands the Old Tolbooth Kirk, whose blackened Gothic spire, designed by the English architect, Augustus Pugin, stretches 240 ft (75 m) into the sky, and is the highest point in the city. From the outside it is still very much a church, but step inside and your eyes are dazzled by an almost psychedelic brightness, with walls painted purple, lime and citrus yellow. For the ghosts of congregations past who sat

through sermons in Gaelic it must have been a shock to now find themselves in The Hub, the new nerve centre of the Edinburgh Festival. The building's reincarnation after years of lying empty was completed in 1999.

Looking across Old Town rooftops to Calton Hill

The Lawnmarket

The Royal Mile becomes the Lawnmarket at this point, and is joined by Johnston Terrace, the street which curves up the south side of Castle Rock. Before the terrace was built in the nineteenth century, the only access from the south was via the Upper Bow, up the steep cobbles from the Grassmarket below. There was once a system of rope pulleys where there are now steps, to help drag the heavily laden, horse-drawn carts up the steep cobbles. It was hereabouts that Major Weir, a lay preacher and Commander of the Town Guard, lived a secret life of incest, bestiality and sorcery with his sister Grizel, something he confessed to at the age of 70. He was taken down the Royal Mile to the Tolbooth jail and sentenced to be strangled and burnt in 1670. At his sister's execution, the crowd were amazed to see her struggling to throw off her clothes 'that she might die with all the shame she could.' It is said that Grizel's ghost with its charred flesh and ghoulish grin still haunts the area, and that her brother's ghost may suddenly appear galloping down the High Street on a headless black horse surrounded by flames.

We are now among the towering tenements and their rabbit-warren of dank narrow alleyways – the Old Town's famous closes, of which there are now around 60 where there were once over 300. Many were named after their residents, though as these changed the names sometimes followed suit. One of the first closes, just below the Outlook Tower, leads to Milne's Court, built in 1690 for Robert Mylne, Charles II's Master Mason. It was converted into accommodation for Edinburgh University students in 1971. Other close names reflected particular lines of business, such as Advocates' Close or Fishmarket Close. There was even a Stinking Close! But the names were all by word of mouth, since it was only in 1790 that the Town Council insisted on street signs. For visitors, the only answer was to rely on one of the Old Town guides, known as 'caddies', who could navigate their way through the maze, perhaps by sense of smell. People had been complaining about the stench of 'Auld Reekie' since the early sixteenth century and with a rising population and inadequate drainage things were bound to get worse.

Milne's Court

As darkness fell in the city, the closes would echo with that most feared of street cries, 'gardy-loo!' – a warning that a shower of filth was about to rain down from on high. In response the caddies would shout back, 'Hud yer haunde!' to win a moment's cease-fire as they scuttled for cover. Residents were supposed to desist from flinging the contents of chamber pots out of their windows and instead

James' Court

take their waste to one of 20 muck carts provided by the council. In practice this prototype wheely-bin was often ignored. And for pedestrians like Jonathan Swift the problem did not end at night: 'A man that walks through Edinburgh streets in a morning is as careful as he can to watch diligently, and spy out for filth in his way. Not that he is curious to observe...it, but only with a design to come out as cleanly as he may.'

For women the solution was to wear a pair of overshoes made of wood, leather and iron known as pattens.

By 1690 there were almost 22,000 people living in Edinburgh, most of them crammed into the Old Town tenements which, for want of space, began to grow ever taller until becoming, in the words of Robert Louis Stevenson, 'smoky beehives ten stories high'. An earlier statute limiting the number to five was clearly ignored. Each building was divided vertically by thick partition walls into what were called 'Lands' – hence the term 'landmarket', or 'Lawnmarket' as it became. These blocks were split into houses – one per floor. Those at the front, looking onto the Royal Mile, enjoyed reasonable daylight; those tucked down the back of the close must have been gloomy beyond words. With judges, tradesmen, paupers and wealthy merchants living cheek by jowl there was a remarkable social mix. Some floors were more desirable than others, however, as we shall discover at Gladstone's Land.

This sixteenth-century building on the North side of the Lawnmarket had been condemned for demolition when the National Trust for Scotland bought it for £762 in 1934 and embarked on the slow, painstaking business of restoration. It was originally bought in 1617 by Thomas Gledstanes, a merchant from Kirkcudbright, who set about

Gladstone's Land

immediately extending the property 23 ft (7 m) into the Royal Mile. Considering all other householders in the street had done or were about to do the same, the width of what was then the 'Kingis Hie Street' shrank considerably.

The Lawnmarket

Gledstanes seems to have kept the third floor for himself and rented out the others as self-contained flats. The ground floor was probably let to a tradesman selling homespun woollen cloth and linen from a small booth which was open to the pavement. Beside this there would have been a cruive, or pen, for a pig which could forage in the street, and an outside flight of stairs connecting the pavement to the living quarters above, which rose five storeys to the cheapest accommodation in the attic.

To form a picture of the Lawnmarket in the seventeenth century, one can take the front of Gladstone's Land and duplicate it down the street. Then place a line of wooden pillars on the pavement, attach a roof and balconies above and you have created an attractive arcade. One has to ask

why they were ever swept away. In other cities such as Bologna one can still enjoy strolling along porticoed streets completely sheltered from the elements – why not in Edinburgh, where the weather is ten times worse? As Stevenson wrote, 'The delicate did die early, and I as a survivor among the bleak winds and plumping rain have sometimes been tempted to envy their fate.'

The words of Stevenson, and those of Robert Burns, Sir Walter Scott and the poet Robert Fergusson, live on in the Writers' Museum in Lady Stair's Close a few doors down. The house was built for Sir William Gray in 1622 and incorporated a pair of ankle-twisting trip steps to foil would-be intruders. There was an allotment at the back that sloped down to the Nor' Loch.

Across the street is first Riddle's Court, where the eighteenth-century philosopher David Hume once lived, and then Brodie's Close, the home of William Brodie, the real-life basis of Robert Louis Stevenson's story *Dr Jekyll and Mr Hyde*. Outwardly pious and respected as a Deacon of the City, he was always short of money to support a passion for gambling, two mistresses and the families they bore him. The solution was to keep a wad of putty in his hand and make a surreptitious imprint of the keys of the tradesmen he visited during the day. By night, armed with a replica key forged by his tame blacksmith, he could return and help himself. He was finally arrested in Amsterdam and sentenced to be hanged outside the Old Tolbooth in 1788. It was rumoured that Brodie had wired his body to soften the drop and had inserted a metal tube down his throat to avoid suffocation. In any event it

Wardrop's Court & Lady Stair's Close

took three attempts until he was pronounced dead.

Edinburgh's last public execution took place just beyond here in 1864, on the corner of George IV Bridge; the site is marked by three brass plates in the road.

Deacon Brodie's Tavern on the Lawnmarket

The High Street

At this point the Royal Mile becomes known as The High Street, which bulges outwards to form what was once the

hub of the nation, containing the seat of government, the Cathedral and the Law Courts. This was also the site of the original Tolbooth, marked by a heart-shaped pattern of granite setts (stones) embedded in the road. In its time it had been a courthouse, a Council Chamber, a prison – immortalised by Sir Walter Scott in *The Heart of Midlothian* – and a place of execution. It had stood for over 400 years by the time it was pulled down in 1817.

The Parliament, with its fine seventeenth-century hammer-beam roof and stained-glass windows, sat from 1639 until it was dissolved in 1707 with the Act of Union. As the politicians moved out the lawyers moved in and the building remains an adjunct to the Law Courts. Across the

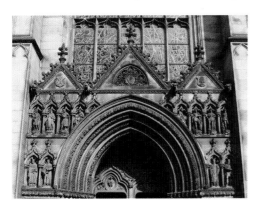

St Giles' Cathedral – West Door

street are the City Chambers, designed in 1753 by the architect John Adam as the Royal Exchange, though it never really caught on with the merchants, who preferred to conduct their business in the street. It is a beautifully proportioned building with an elegant square and porticoed façade, but seems curiously out of place, as though it were an embassy from the New Town.

Looming up above, with its giant crown-shaped steeple, is the Cathedral of St Giles, the patron saint of beggars and criminals. The present building is less than 200 years old, though there has been a church on this site since the

David Hume statue

ninth century. It is not a thing of any beauty and as the writer Jim Crumley put it, '...it seems a darkly unemotional Kirk within.' It is hard to imagine it once ringing with the fiery, pulpit-thumping sermons of John Knox, the great sixteenth-century Protestant reformer. In those days St Giles' was surrounded by stalls selling meat, groceries and bread, and by Luckenbooths, or 'locked booths', which became the centre of the jewellery trade. The street would have been packed with people, shopping and gossiping around the old

Mercat Cross

Mercat Cross. It was here that Royal Proclamations were read and the occasional VIP was hanged, like the Marquis of Montrose in 1650. As one proud citizen declared, long before the New Town was conceived, 'Here I stand at what is called the Cross of Edinburgh, and can in a few minutes take 50 men of genius and learning by the hand.'

Not everyone liked the throng, however, especially since the market stalls squeezed the Royal Mile to just 15 ft (4.5 m) wide. 'This would undoubtedly be one of the noblest streets in Europe, if an ugly mass of mean buildings, called Luckenbooths, had not thrust itself by what accident I

The colourful Festival Fringe office on the High Street

know not, into the middle of the way', grumbled Tobias Smollett in 1776. Compared to now, it would have felt much more hemmed in by tenements some 14 storeys high.

The rising buildings could never keep up with the increasing population, which was being crammed into less and less space. With this real and growing sense of claustrophobia came the fear of fire, plague and of being crushed when the masonry collapsed, as it did from time to time. One fire near St Giles' left over 400 families homeless, and another blaze destroyed the Tron Kirk steeple, sending molten lead

Street theatre at Festival time

flowing through the streets. Houses that had been struck by the plague were often closed up and abandoned, as if to

Festive flags and the Tron Kirk on the High Street

contain any disease that still lurked there. As Stevenson wrote, '...what a terrible next-door neighbour for superstitious citizens!'

Further down the High Street, opposite Stevenlaw's Close, is the site of the old Guard House, a long, black-slated single-storey building that housed the Edinburgh Town Guard, which was eventually replaced by a modern police force in 1817. They had a novel approach to certain crimes: anyone caught drunk in public was taken to the Guard House and forced to sit astride a wooden horse that stood outside, with their feet strapped together and a drinking cup tied to their head. It all provided good entertainment for the crowds.

Just beyond is the old Tron Kirk, where New Year revellers still gather at Hogmanay. It contains some interesting medieval remains. From the slim Gothic spire above there once hung a set of bells, whose ringing drove some to distraction. 'That wanwordy, crazy, dinsome thing!' cried the poet Fergusson.

Here we reach the intersection with the North and South Bridges. In 1767 the young architect James Craig submitted plans for a New Town to be built on land north of the Castle. In contrast to the ramshackle tenements and dark, fetid closes this was to be a monument to symmetrical purity, full of wide avenues,

Crowne Plaza Hotel – built in 1989

imposing squares and graceful crescents. Six years later, the North Bridge was flung out over the Nor' Loch to connect the Royal Mile on its high ridge to the promised land

beyond. Those with means could scarcely wait to swap the claustrophobic Old Town for the Georgian splendour of the New. Edinburgh would never be the same again.

A little further on is Bailie Fyfe's Close, where one Sunday morning in 1863 an ancient tenement, 'a building rotten to the core', simply sank to the ground. Thirty-five people were killed and the gap in the city outline, like a missing tooth, could be seen for many miles. Next door, down Chalmers Close, is a new Brass Rubbing Centre beside the ruins of a once-

John Knox House (above), with James Mossman's coat of arms (below)

beautiful medieval church, which was demolished in 1848,
to make room for Waverley railway station.

Continuing down the hill we come to two of the oldest

dwellings in Edinburgh.
Moubray House dates back to
the mid fifteenth century and
at one time or another has
been home to the writer
Daniel Defoe, a popular
tavern and a temperance
hotel. John Knox House,
next door, gives a fair

impression of what the houses would have looked like at the time of Mary Queen of Scots, in the sixteenth century, with its outside flight of steps and timbered galleries. The house belonged to James Mossman, the Queen's goldsmith and keeper of the Mint. Like Sir William Kirkcaldy, who held the Castle for Mary during the Lang Siege until forced to surrender, Mossman was caught on the wrong side. Together they were drawn backwards down the Royal Mile to the Mercat Cross where they were hanged in 1573. Whether Knox, the great crusader against 'the puddle of popery' and author of *The Monstrous Regiment of Women*, ever lived here is a matter of doubt.

Across the street is the Museum of Childhood, 'the noisiest museum in the world', whose collection stretches from Victorian dolls and puzzles to a video history of 'Thunderbirds'. Beside it stands Tweeddale Court, named after the Marquis of Tweeddale. According to Daniel Defoe it was one of the most princely buildings in the city with its terraced gardens down to the Cowgate. It later became the Head Office of

Tweeddale Court

the British Linen Bank, and between 1817 and 1973 was the home of the publishers, Oliver and Boyd.

The Canongate

As you leave the High Street, heading east into the Canongate, you notice the transition from rattling cobbles to smooth tarmac, and how the road becomes a little narrower and steeper. You might also sense a vague shift in tone away from the tourist souvenir shops higher up to those selling hand-knitted jumpers, old maps and second-hand books. Other than that, it all feels very much one and the same street.

Bible Land, Canongate

Back in the days when this was a walled city, however, Edinburgh and the Canongate were two separate burghs, and this is where the old Netherbow Port stood, one of the six gateways into the city. It was built in 1513, and its outline can be seen, marked by brass insets in the road. Contemporary drawings show it to have been three storeys high, with a tall spire and battlements that were occasionally decorated with the heads of criminals and preachers. If need arose, the central portcullis could be quickly dropped, sealing off the city from the outside. At such moments the Canongate, which was only incorporated into the Royal Burgh of Edinburgh in 1856, must have felt extremely vulnerable. And as if to emphasise this sense that life beyond the city walls was something beyond the pale, the last close in the High Street is called World's End Close. The Netherbow Port was demolished in 1764, and today, near the site, the Netherbow lives on as an arts centre and theatre.

The Canongate's name derives from the Augustinian canons of Holyrood who were given permission by King David I to build on either side of their 'gait', or walk, which led up from the Abbey. It remained a quiet hamlet until King James IV began building the Palace of Holyrood in 1501, which prompted his courtiers to migrate down the

hill and build their mansions nearby. The trend continued as Holyrood evolved into the official royal residence to replace 'that windy and right unpleasant castle', as James V called it.

This part of the Royal Mile feels more residential, with Chessel's Court, a 1960s renovation of an eighteenth-century mansion block, whose green courtyard is almost unique in the Old Town. It was around here that Deacon Brodie made his ill-conceived raid on the General Excise Office that eventually led to his arrest.

The building opposite is mysteriously called Morocco Land, a name apparently derived from its life-size statue of a Moor. According to legend, its origins concern the daughter of a seventeenth-century Lord Provost who may

have been in the harem of the Sultan of Morocco.

Further down the hill stands Moray House, with its tall, sloping roof and balcony. Behind here were once the most beautiful gardens which contained a summer house, where in 1707 the final signatures to the Treaty of Union were added by a 'parcel of rogues' cowering from the mob.

Continuing down the hill you reach a pair of museums, almost facing each other – The People's Story and The Museum of Edinburgh. The former is, as its name suggests, a history of everyday life in the city, housed in the old

Canongate Tolbooth, which has been a council chamber, a courthouse and overspill accommodation for Calton Jail. Here you can eavesdrop on the conversation in a 1940s wartime kitchen, peek into an old prison cell, pick up the gossip from a 1950s tea-room and get a taste of what the Old Town was like in the nineteenth and twentieth centuries.

Canongate Tolbooth

The population in this part of Edinburgh peaked in the middle of the nineteenth century at 50,000, eight times the present level, and most were living in abject poverty, the wealthier citizens having moved to the New Town. 'Times are changed,' wrote Stevenson, where once there was 'not so much as a blade of grass between rich and poor. [Now] two score families herd together [in] discomfort from foundation to chimney tops with an air of sluttishness and dirt. In the first room a birth, in another a death.' A swarm of righteous Victorians descended on the Canongate to see for themselves. 'Human beings are living in a state worse than brutes,' wrote one. 'They have gravitated to a point of wretchedness [from] which no effort from the pulpit, the press or the schoolroom can raise them'.

The Museum of Edinburgh (formerly Huntly House Museum) focuses on an earlier, pre-New Town history of Edinburgh. The building

was originally built for John Acheson in 1570 and was typical of the houses here, with its white, gabled upper floor projecting over the street. It seems Acheson was aware that his fine mansion might inspire jealousy. He hung a tablet outside which, loosely translated from the Latin, reads: 'I'm a happy man today, your turn may come tomorrow, so what's your problem?'. Behind, through an immensely thick archway that could be sealed off in times of danger, lies one of the prettiest closes in the Royal Mile. Bakehouse Close seems to preserve, better than most, the original idea of a close being a separate street on its own. In 1851 it was recorded that 230 people were living here.

The Canongate Kirk, facing you across the street, certainly differs from other churches we have passed and provides a welcome relief from the blackened, Gothic spires that punctuate the sky. Others disagree; 'A most unpicturesque-looking edifice of nameless style', sniffed James Grant in his *Old and New Edinburgh*. It was built in 1688 by James VII of Scotland, and II of England, the year he was swept off the throne.

Canongate Kirk

Whatever one's view of the kirk, there is an impressive congregation of gravestones gathered here in the Royal Mile's only graveyard. Here lies Adam Smith, author of *The Wealth of Nations*, the poet Robert Fergusson, and George Drummond, six times Lord Provost from 1725 to 1760. These were later joined by the architect Robert Hurd, who died in 1963, after years devoted to carrying on the restoration work of Robert Geddes and extending it to the Canongate. Without their commitment to saving and preserving what remained of the Old Town after a century of neglect, the Royal Mile would be a shadow of what it is today. Often they were battling against an establishment view that the street was almost beyond redemption, that the only hope was to flatten what remained and start again.

Next door, Dunbar's Close is a secluded oasis from the bustle of the street with its garden donated to the City by the Mushroom Trust in 1978 and laid out in a seventeenth-century style. On the other side of the Canongate, in Crighton's Close, is the modern home of the Scottish Poetry Library.

Continuing on we reach Brown's Close or 'Golfer's Land', designated by a bronze plaque on the wall. Above it is a coat of arms displaying a raised fist clutching a golf club over a shield decorated with stars and pelicans. The story goes that the Duke of York, later James VII, was challenged to a round of golf on Leith Links by two English nobles staying at Holyrood. The outcome would determine who invented the ancient game, whether it was an Englishman or a Scot. James chose John Patterson, an impoverished cobbler and maker of leather golf balls, as his partner. Needless to say the English were soundly thrashed, and Patterson was given enough prize money to build his house. The trouble is, 'Golfer's Land' was built in 1601, 80 years before the match was played. Perhaps the tale was dreamt up in Jenny Ha's tavern next door, famous for its claret and its Younger's Edinburgh Ale, whose strength could 'glue the drinker's lips together.' Despite an ancient law forbidding women from working in taverns and drinking shops, being 'a great snare to the Youth and occasion for Loudness and Debauchery', Jenny Ha's survived until 1857.

Having now reached the bottom of the Canongate, opposite the new Scottish Parliament, we come to one last tavern, one of the 240 recorded in a survey of 1740 along with 52 brothels. The White Horse Inn was either named after Mary Queen of Scots' famous white palfrey,

or the nag that won the Inn's owner a hefty bet during a day's racing at Leith Sands. Either way it became the main terminus for stagecoaches on the eight-day journey to and from London. Demolished in 1868, its name lives on as a major brand of Scotch

White Horse Close

whisky. The picturesque early seventeenth-century White Horse Close with its flower pots, flag-stoned courtyard and steep gables, was heavily restored in 1962.

Our journey down the Royal Mile takes us past the new Scottish Parliament. Its Spanish architect, Enric Miralles, died before his vision of the parliament's buildings, like a cluster of upturned boats, took shape. Let's hope its walls of dark slate and granite and its roofs of stainless steel age well in Edinburgh's 'bleak winds and plumping rain'. Opposite the new parliament buildings, at the entrance to the Palace of Holyroodhouse in Horse Wynd, is the new Queen's Gallery which opened in 2002. This specially designed facility is the first permanent exhibition space for the Royal Collection in Scotland.

The royal arms of James V, Abbey Strand

Finally, at the very foot of the Royal Mile stands the Abbey and Palace of Holyroodhouse. Legend has it that

King David I was hunting here in 1128 when he was thrown from his horse and charged by a stag. The king grabbed its antlers, at which point the stag disappeared, leaving him

holding a crucifix. To thank God for his escape, King David had an Augustinian abbey built on the spot. The name 'Holyrood' comes from the word 'rood' or cross. The ruins of the Abbey remain and were said to have been the inspiration for Mendelssohn's Scottish Symphony after his visit of 1829.

The Palace of Holyroodhouse began life as the Abbey's

Holyrood Abbey

guesthouse, until James IV turned it into a Royal Palace in the early sixteenth century. It was greatly expanded over the next 300 years, to give it its quasi-baronial appearance. All that remains of the original Palace is the northwest tower, where Mary Queen of Scots had her apartments, and where her personal secretary, David Rizzio, was stabbed to death in 1566.

From here it is only a mile to the Castle, but what a feast lies in between.

The Palace of Holyroodhouse